Time Management

The Definitive Manual On Time Management: Strategies For Achieving Productivity And Conquering Procrastination

(Effective Time Management, Enhanced Productivity, Increased Motivation, And Successful Task Completion)

LubomirJagła

TABLE OF CONTENT

Managing Time in Teams and Projects 1

Incorporate Time Management Into Every Aspect of Your Life: 8

Effective Problem-Solving and Decision-Making 30

Constraints with the Conventional Time Management Method 50

What Are the Principal Difficulties and Barriers to Productivity and Time Management? 72

Techniques for balancing work and life 98

Medication 124

Managing Time in Teams and Projects

It's critical to plan and work with teams and projects and manage your time.

The following are some methods for efficiently managing team time:

Unambiguous Communication: Create effective and transparent communication channels to promote cooperation and information exchange.

What is meant by realistic deadlines? Establish reasonable timelines for tasks and projects when working as a team, keeping in mind the team's capabilities and the availability of resources.

Effective Gatherings: Establish a defined agenda and a time limit to help you run well-organized and productive meetings.

Ensure that every conversation advances the project and is pertinent.

By putting particular tactics into practice to handle workloads and increase productivity, you'll build strong groundwork for obtaining significant outcomes.

The following chapters will cover strategies for improving time management on a personal level and striking a healthy balance between work and personal life.

Prepare to change your workspace into a more effective and productive one.

Individual Time Scheduling

The Value of Individual Time Management

In order to practice self-care and maintain a healthy work-life balance, one must be proficient in time management.

This chapter will look at doable tactics to help you maximize your time daily.

Making Self-Care a Priority

Taking care of yourself is essential to keeping your personal life in balance.

Here are some strategies to make self-care a priority in your everyday schedule:

Set Aside Time for Yourself:

Allocate time for enjoyable pursuits that revitalize you, such as physical activity, mindfulness, hobbies, or reading.

These rest periods are crucial for reviving energy and lowering stress levels.

Establish Boundaries: Define boundaries between your personal and professional lives.

Don't bring work home with you; schedule some time to unplug from social media and electronics.

Get Enough Sleep: To maintain the health of your body and mind, prioritize a restful night's sleep.

Create a restful atmosphere and stick to a regular sleep schedule.

Individual Structure

The key to maximizing your time is effective organization.

Here are some tips to keep you organized:

Employ a Calendar or Planner: To keep track of appointments, chores, and personal objectives, use a planner or organizer.

Sort your tasks into priority lists and allot time for each.

Create To-Do Lists: Make your tasks daily or weekly.

Marking tasks as completed will help you feel accomplished as you finish them.

Control Your Money: Give your own money, including your investments, expenses, and budget, some thought.

This will assist you in avoiding financial strain and preserving personal equilibrium.

Establishing Limits and Saying "No"

Effective personal time management requires the ability to say "no" and to set appropriate boundaries.

Several pointers

Make your responsibilities a priority: Examine your requests and appointments with great care.

Pay attention to what matters most and is consistent with your objectives.

Define Reasonable Boundaries: Establish precise time and energy limits.

Avoid overcommitting your time or taking on more work than you can handle.

Daily Practice of Personal Time Management

Developing dependable habits is essential to practicing personal time management.

Here are some methods to include time management into your everyday schedule:

Establish Daily Objectives: Make attainable goals for every day.

This will support you in maintaining concentration and concentrating your efforts on the most important tasks.

Use Free Time Sensibly: Utilize all your daily breaks and downtime.

Use them quickly, like responding to emails or taking a stretch break.

Incorporate Time Management Into Every Aspect of Your Life:

Use time management techniques in all facets of your life, such as leisure, relationships, and self-care.

I hope this chapter has clarified time management in your personal life.

You can lay the groundwork for a well-rounded and satisfying existence by balancing your personal, family, and recreational pursuits.

An action plan should include a resource identification section to help you reach your goal. This could involve material resources like project financing or human resources like a group of workers or volunteers. Knowing ahead of time what resources you'll need will help you budget and prepare appropriately and assist you in spotting any obstacles you might encounter along the way.

Your goal if you have a defined objective, a schedule, and a list of available resources. A strategy is a plan of action or measures you will follow to accomplish your objective. These could involve activities like networking, training, or research. It's critical to be as specific as possible while creating a strategy and note any potential difficulties or roadblocks you may encounter.

Once you have a well-thought-out plan, executing and carrying it out is critical. Due to the need for commitment and discipline, this is frequently the most challenging step in the process. Establishing regular check-ins or progress updates and making any adjustments to your plan will help you stay on track.

A strong communication strategy must also be in place to inform all parties involved of the project's status and any problems.

Creating an action plan is a crucial first step toward accomplishing any aim or target. You may improve your chances of success by clearly stating your objectives, setting up a schedule, determining your resources, formulating a plan, carrying it out, and keeping an eye on it. Recall that creating a plan of action is a continuous process that should be evaluated, updated, and modified as necessary. You may improve your chances of succeeding by being focused, organized, and on course with a well-thought-out plan in place.

There once was a young lady named Sarah who was constantly dreaming of opening her own company. She wanted to pursue her passion for fashion as a career, as she had always been interested in it and had a knack for design. But she had never done the work to make her goal a reality.

One day, Sarah decided she could no longer wait for the right chance to present itself. She understood that she would need to act if she was going to accomplish her aim. She was aware of creating an action plan.

Sarah started by outlining her objective precisely. Her goal was to launch a fashion design company that focused on producing ethically and sustainably produced clothes. Although she knew this was a lofty objective, she was committed to achieving it.

Sarah made a timetable after she was sure about her objective. Within the year, she set a goal to function fully in her firm. She divided the objective into smaller, more doable tasks, like networking, industry research, and business plan development.

Sarah then determined what tools she would require to fulfill her mission. She started looking into other funding alternatives, including grants, loans, and crowdsourcing, since she knew she would need money to launch her firm.

She also understood that to handle all the different facets of her firm, she would require a group of people.

Sarah started to plan her approach to reaching her goal after considering her resources, timeframe, and objective. She spent a lot of time reading about the fashion industry and sustainable fashion methods because she realized that research would be an important part of her plan. She also started attending business events, networking with industry individuals, and contacting possible mentors.

Sarah got her plan in place and started moving. In order to raise money for her company, she launched a crowdfunding campaign and applied for grants and loans. She also started having meetings with possible team members, and eventually, she put together a group of gifted and driven people who agreed with her goal.

Sarah put forth much effort over the following year to achieve her goal. Despite the numerous obstacles she faced, she never gave up. She was committed to reaching her objective and was driven to see her company succeed.

After a year of diligence and determination, Sarah was finally prepared to open for business. She started her own fashion design company, specializing in clothes manufactured with ethical and sustainable practices. Her company took off, and she soon became known as a pioneer in the sustainable fashion sector. Sarah's tale serves as a reminder that reaching a goal takes great effort and commitment. However, everything is achievable if you have a well-defined objective, a thoughtful action plan, and the resolve to pursue it.

Setting priorities and maintaining focus: After creating a plan of action, you must rank your tasks and focus on the most crucial ones. This ensures that you are not squandering time or effort on unimportant chores and are moving closer to your most crucial objectives.

Setting priorities and maintaining concentration is critical for success in both personal and professional spheres.

They enable people to reach their objectives in a productive and well-organized way and to manage their time and energy efficiently.

It's critical to determine your goals and objectives to prioritize tasks and maintain focus. This entails setting short- and long-term objectives and figuring out what jobs and pursuits will get you there. You can start setting priorities for your chores once you know your goals.

The Eisenhower matrix, which divides jobs into four quadrants according to their importance and urgency, is useful for task prioritization. Important and urgent tasks should be accomplished as soon as feasible and given the highest priority. Important but non-urgent tasks should also be prioritized and planned ahead of time on your calendar. As much as possible, urgent but not crucial tasks should be assigned to others. Additionally, non-urgent or non-important jobs ought to be completely dropped.

Controlling distractions is a crucial component of maintaining focus. Many other types of distractions include social media, email, phone notifications, and other people's interruptions. Setting limits and creating a dedicated, distraction-free workspace reduces distractions. Disabling notifications and designating particular times of the day to monitor and reply to texts and emails are also beneficial.

The Pomodoro Method is an additional method for maintaining attention that divides work into 25-minute segments and takes a 5-minute rest in between. This enables you to concentrate on a particular subject briefly before taking a break to clear your head and refocus.

It's also critical to monitor your energy levels throughout the day and to plan your most demanding and significant chores for when you're most energetic. It's also critical to take pauses and partake in rejuvenating activities for your body and mind, like working out, practicing meditation, or hanging out with loved ones.

Setting priorities and maintaining focus might be difficult, but they can be mastered with some work and discipline. You may accomplish your objectives and be productive by defining clear goals, prioritizing chores, controlling distractions, and being aware of your energy levels.

Setting priorities and maintaining concentration is essential for accomplishing our objectives and leading fulfilling lives. It calls for self-awareness, discipline, and efficient time management. You may assist yourself in becoming more focused and productive by being aware of your priorities and trying to get rid of distractions and procrastination. You'll be able to accomplish your objectives and live a more satisfying life.

Technologies and Tools for Time Management

In the age of technological advancement, where digital innovation permeates every aspect of our lives, it makes sense that we embrace tools and technologies that improve our time management abilities. Let's explore the wealth of digital tools available to us as we enter the world of contemporary time management and see how they can completely transform how we approach our assignments and objectives.

Taking Advantage of Digital

Imagine having a virtual to-do list that syncs with your devices, a digital assistant who never forgets your meetings, and a project management tool. These are a few examples of what's available in time management software. Software and programs that not only simplify our lives but also increase our productivity thanks to the digital era.

Using Calendar Apps to Manage Your Schedule

A well-organized timetable is one of the fundamental elements of good time management. Calendar programs such as Apple Calendar, Microsoft Outlook, and Google Calendar have progressed beyond basic date-tracking. They have now integrated task lists, reminders, and color-coded events. With the help of these apps, you may precisely plan your days rather than merely recording activities.

Software for Project Management: Team Up and Win

Project management software has become a useful tool for anyone juggling the complexities of collaboration and project deadlines. A consolidated platform for assigning tasks, monitoring progress, and collaborating is offered by apps like Monday.com, Asana, and Trello. Tasks set deadlines and see how each project is progressing in real-time.

Apps for Task Management: From To-Do to Ta-Da!

Envision possessing an ever-evolving to-do list that adjusts to your priorities. That's what task management apps like Wunderlist (now part of Microsoft To Do), Any.Do, and Todoist offer. With functions like categories, recurrent assignments, and due dates, these applications turn your to-do list from a simple checklist into a calculated road map for achievement.

Tools for Tracking Time: Managing the Temporal Landscape

Have you ever wondered where time goes? By monitoring your digital activity, time-tracking apps like RescueTime and Toggl let you gain insights into your usage patterns. It's like having a magnifying glass over your everyday activities to assist you in spotting time wasters and bad behaviors that require changing.

Apps for Meditation and Mindfulness: Discovering Your Zen

In the middle of the hustle and bustle. Apps for mindfulness and meditation, such as Calm and Headspace, lead you through relaxation techniques to help you better focus and manage stress. Including these mindful moments in your daily routine fosters a comprehensive sense of well-being rather than merely time management.

Accept the Harmony of Technology

It's crucial to remember that, even as we embrace the digital symphony of time management tools and technologies, you are the conductor, and they are the instruments. Select the best tools for you and smoothly incorporate them into your daily routine. The idea is to use technology to extend your capabilities rather than to become a slave to it.

The Delegation Art

The ability to assign work when and how it is needed is essential for efficient time management. The art of delegation is a masterpiece in the broad time management scheme. Envision increasing your output, sharpening your focus, and giving your team more authority by deftly passing the torch. Rather than assigning work to others, delegation is about coordinating a harmonious blend of productivity and teamwork.

The Delegation Conundrum: Taking Up the Mantle

Realizing that you can't do everything is the first step towards being an expert delegate. Falling into the trap of trying to multitask wears you out and lowers your productivity. This is where delegation becomes an ally in your time management strategy, assisting you in allocating tasks to the most qualified people.

Interpreting Delegatable Assignments

When it comes to delegation, not every task is made equal. The secret is identifying the jobs that can be efficiently delegated without sacrificing quality. Delegating is best suited for routine and repetitive activities, administrative responsibilities, and specialized initiatives that play to the strengths of others. You can free up critical bandwidth for projects that require your specialized skill set by giving up these activities.

The Dance of Delegation: Selecting Appropriate Partners

Consider a jigsaw puzzle where every piece fits perfectly to form the finished image. The correct partners are the missing components in the world of delegation. Choosing people with the right expertise, abilities, and motivation for the job is important. Delegation is giving responsibilities to others who can do things better rather than just unloading work to them.

Effective Problem-Solving and Decision-Making

The excessive variety that any choice could have been faced with has been a problem that has prevented many colleagues. I rarely give it much thought, but before deciding what to buy, I have to make a few decisions when I visit my favorite sandwich store! And even when I get there, there are hundreds, if not thousands, of things to choose from! Don't let the limitless options depress you. Instead, learn how to solve problems systematically.

Which protocol, though, is the best? I'll give you some thoughts and illustrations. But ideally, you will design your framework. This gives you room to expand it to the extent that you require. Your knowledge and the answers you've picked up from others will inform it. One such framework is the one put out by Martin G. Moore. In a brief piece, he provided insight into the eight components of an excellent decision. These are the following:

A reliable source Trust is fostered by responsibility. Furthermore, it improves your leadership abilities. Rejection is nothing to be afraid of and trust your instincts.

Sources close to the focus point: Those closest to the issue typically hold the most important knowledge.

Pursuing the fundamental cause should be the goal. However, there are situations where treating some symptoms is more important than addressing the source. But generally speaking, focus on the root of the issue. It will frequently treat the symptoms subtly.

Evaluation of several points of view: It is not expected of a leader to grasp every issue they encounter right away. Find the people who can give you pertinent insights and use them to your advantage to make a wiser decision.

An overview of the possible effects: Engage in attentive practice.

Recognize that your choice will result in changes.

If you don't experience recurrent anxiety, list a few potential problems. You may be better equipped to handle those setbacks as a result.

Striking a balance between immediate and long-term benefits: Ignoring long-term consequences in favor of immediate gain is a problem that many leaders encounter. Although the latter appears elegant and polished for your yearly delivery, it is not worthwhile to ignore its long-term usefulness entirely. Keeping both in balance will result in the best choices.

A promise to keep all parties informed: Please note that you are not seeking approval. This step's goal is much more altruistic. You want everyone who is involved to know the facts. They will be able to smoothly execute your decision as a result.

A prompt delivery: You'll be more nimble without a strong framework. This point aims to cut down on how long it takes to travel through the flowchart. For instance, follow your instincts if four knowledgeable sources offer contradicting advice. Consider carefully before assuming that everyone agrees.

Moore ignores what I believe to be the most crucial component: setting priorities. As we did with our objectives and time earlier, choices can be important or insignificant. Redistributing firm resources is not the same as deciding who will bring what to the office Thanksgiving potluck. Decide what's vital and urgent first. I would advise making judgments one at a time if you have several equally important to make. Multitasking is a wild goose chase, as I said in passing earlier in this chapter. We become far less concentrated and efficient as a result. If we're attempting to make the right choice, this is awful!

Interestingly, this works well with an Eisenhower matrix. Work-related decisions are unlikely to land in the

Disregard quadrant, but you can arrange your impending discussions in any of the three other places. It will centeraround the aims of your team rather than being relevant to your own goals. The majority of the urgency won't alter. In light of this, think about writing a few instances. By offering this recommendation, I hope to normalize the process of setting priorities for decisions.

The reliable flowchart is another popular structure for setting priorities and resolving issues. This is especially helpful in cases where specific crisis protocols are established. This includes any procedures you decide to implement following observation. When using a flowchart to tackle a problem, begin broadly. "What is the problem?" and "Do I have enough information to act?" are excellent places to start. From there, take appropriate branching. I would rather have a single primary path with satisfying conclusions at each node. In the last case, the conclusion would have been, "Ask relevant parties for information and their opinion," if I didn't have enough details. As you proceed, your main path should become more focused. You may inquire in your second question if you have ever handled a situation like this. If not, "Do you have the right tools to address the root cause?" could appear on the third node. And so forth.

Be adaptable despite all of this planning advice. There are times when a decision becomes void before it's even finished. Or when you suddenly find yourself having to make the most important decision. Make use of more than merely adaptability if at all possible. Provide proactive solutions. Allocate time for unforeseen circumstances. It's time to examine proactive time management techniques.

Reducing DisruptionsIndividual Disruptions

Employee Disruptions

Inform managers and important staff that you cannot be bothered unless there is an emergency. Give them a definition of an emergency by compiling a list of precise instances. Since "emergency" has a broad sense, it should be quite clear. Some only consider fire or impending death to be emergencies. Some people view a paper jam in the copier as an emergency.

Next, depending on how frequently they now contact you, arrange appointments with each person daily or weekly. If you and your manager regularly converse throughout the day, set a specific time. People are less likely to interrupt you if they know their allotted time and what constitutes an emergency.

Clients and Customers

Small business owners frequently unintentionally teach their consumers and customers to interrupt them. Customers come to expect the kind of service you offer, even though serving them is your top priority. Your company has frequently set its expectations. They may be accustomed to receiving your phone calls at any time, without charge, and expecting a prompt response or one that arrives in a certain window of time.

Inform your clients or customers when you schedule your week so that you may answer calls and emails whenever necessary.

Establish guidelines to help you manage the conduct of others.

Establish your definition of client crises and the situations in which you will intervene.

Family Members You can treat your family members in the same way. If your partner usually communicates during your OUT, discuss emergencies and schedule regular conversation times.

A partner will frequently feel more important because of this since they will know you are making time for them specifically.

Devices Human interruptions account for the majority of the disruptions caused by devices. The good news is that we have command over these gadgets. All of them can be momentarily turned off.

Processes Choose the disruptions that are focused on processes from your selection. Make two categories now: avoidable and unpreventable.

It is possible to stop a lot of process interruptions. Computer viruses, low inventory, running out of supplies, etc. The majority of these kinds of disruption ought to be eliminated with a little forethought and the implementation of fresh strategies.

Certain process disruptions cannot be avoided. Equipment failures, cash flow issues, power outages, etc.

Certain unavoidable business disruptions can be "cured."

• Backup generators can prevent power disruptions.

• Having a cash reserve for equipment replacement, backing up computers, having backup equipment, or having solid technical support contacts on staff or retainer can all assist in preventing equipment malfunctions.

- Establishing a line of credit, cash reserves, or credit cards can help alleviate cash flow problems.

Time management apps and tools to increase efficiency and productivity.

Time management and productivity in the digital age we live in. This chapter will examine various tools and apps that help employees and business owners better manage their time.

1. Tools for Time Management

Teams and company executives may stay focused and organized using various time management tools. A few of the most well-known are listed below:

• Todoist offers the capacity to create and assign tasks, set deadlines, and track progress. These features may aid in keeping you and your team organized.

• Calendar apps: Programs like Google Calendar and Outlook help you and your team keep organized by letting you set up appointments, send reminders, and manage your calendar.

• Time-tracking software: Using time-tracking applications like Toggl, Harvest, and RescueTime, you and your team can assess the time spent on each task, identify chances to raise productivity, and identify areas for improvement.

- Email management software: Apps like Boomerang and Inbox by Gmail can help you and your team handle email more efficiently by allowing you to schedule, snooze, and prioritize important communications.

2. Instruments for Automation

Automation solutions can save time for business owners and their staff by automating repetitive tasks. The following are some instances of automation tools:

- Workflow automation tools: Programs like Zapier and IFTTT facilitate workflow automation by letting you create triggers and actions that perform activities like emailing recipients, updating spreadsheets, and creating tasks automatically.

• Social media automation tools: Hootsuite and Buffer, for example, let you schedule posts, monitor mentions on social media, and measure statistics to help you manage your social media accounts more efficiently.

3. Instruments of Communication

The secret to time management success is effective communication. The following tools for communication can keep you and your team in touch:

• Video conferencing tools: By enabling you to host online meetings, webinars, and training sessions, programs like Zoom and Skype can keep you and your staff in touch.

• Apps for instant messaging: By enabling real-time collaboration, file sharing, and instant messaging, apps like Slack and Microsoft Teams can improve team communication.

Actual Cases

Here are a few examples of how technology is being used in the real world to improve time management:

• A software development company uses Asana, a project management platform, to assign tasks and track project progress. They also utilize Toggl to track how much time is spent on different jobs and identify areas where efficiency could be improved.

- A marketing agency uses platforms like Boomerang, Hootsuite, and Slack to plan emails, social media posts, and in-the-moment team communications.
- A freelance writer uses RescueTime to monitor the time spent on each project, Zapier to automate workflows, and Zoom to conduct virtual meetings with clients.

Final Thoughts

Technology has the potential to be a very effective tool for increasing productivity and better time management. Business owners and their teams may stay organized, save time, and work more productively by utilizing time management, automation, and communication solutions. Selecting technology tools that optimize your team's performance and workflow is crucial. Don't forget to remind your staff of the value of technology and to push for regular use of it.

Constraints with the Conventional Time Management Method

1. Having an obsession with perfection

Perfectionism has two drawbacks. Perfectionists want to produce high-quality work and exhibit higher involvement, motivation, and conscientiousness. But their all-or-nothing attitude and rigid, high standards frequently lead to stress, burnout, and worry that hinders their effectiveness.

Time management advice: ● Learn to accept imperfections. While diligence is a positive quality, there are situations when it may consume more time and energy than is necessary. Although it can take a lot of time, paying attention to detail can also be incredibly beneficial. Take a break whenever you notice you are working too hard on a task and ask yourself, "Am I using my time wisely? "Am I producing enough?" Frequently, a few poorly executed activities yield greater outcomes than one activity that fulfills your exacting requirements.

● Regularly assess your progress. Evaluate your work every three weeks, every two weeks, and every month. Could you complete some of the activities with less bother and with little to no negative impact on the final product? Can you recall any chores you overworked or avoided because you feared you wouldn't get it right?

● Release some of your pressure. Give yourself permission to be less perfect and focus on what's vital if you want to do more in less time.

● Seek insight and assistance. Show your boss or supervisor your work frequently to find out if you are making progress and if the quality of your work is enough. If you want to be a more productive employee, be honest about it and be willing to accept feedback.

2. Not Being Able to Focus and Concentrate

The majority of us have, at some point, gone through the feeling of repeatedly reading a paragraph and not being able to understand what it is saying. Or perhaps you have a report or article to write, but you can't focus since your thoughts are racing. Here are a few suggestions to help you get back on course.

Time-management advice:

Recognize your adversaries. Determine which distractions at work affect your capacity to concentrate and operate efficiently. Take the Harvard Business Review's brief exam to find out which distractions most impair your ability to concentrate and to receive advice on how to avoid them.

● Be more attentive to your health. Lack of sleep can easily impair memory, attention, and other cognitive abilities besides concentration. Regular physical activity helps older persons maintain their cognitive health and enhance their focus and attention span. Among the many advantages of mindfulness and meditation are increased focus and concentration.

Make use of your best performance window. Schedule the most difficult chores during the most productive times of the day. Use it wisely and avoid processing emails or phone calls during peak hours.

● Take pauses.

In addition to being enjoyable, breaks can help you mentally recharge, refuel, regain motivation, and lessen decision fatigue. According to research, even 10 minutes of exercise increases focus and performance. Spending time in nature also reduces fatigue.

● Establish daily objectives.

Short-term objectives appeal to our brains for physiological reasons. Dopamine is released by our brains when we accomplish something; this leads to feelings of concentration and motivation to repeat the event.

● Work on multitasking.

Multitasking negatively impacts your focus and performance, including slowing your progress, increasing your risk of making mistakes, stressing you out, and more. As an alternative, concentrate on one task at a time. Committed to the task at hand.

Consult your physician.

Do not dismiss it if you notice a sudden decrease in your capacity to focus, such as difficulty completing everyday tasks, increased errors, or a higher frequency of incorrect decisions. These could be signs of anxiety or depression, and time management techniques can exacerbate the effects of stress on your body, which is currently intolerable, therefore impairing performance.

● Set time limits for social media and the Internet.

3. Ineffective Task Scheduling

A successful time management approach includes efficient scheduling as a key component. Setting incorrect priorities and devoting time to activities that yield minimal or no progress toward your goals will make it impossible for you to focus and manage your time. It doesn't matter if you've mastered the art of setting priorities; an endless cycle of hard and demanding work can lead to stress, anxiety, despair, and burnout. Let's examine how you can divide up your work efficiently.

Time management advice: ● Take into account the Ivy Lee approach. List the top six things you need to get done tomorrow and rank them in order of importance when the day is over. Start working on the most crucial ones the following day.

Prevent the effect of mere hurry. Research indicates that humans are prone to selecting essential jobs with longer-term and more significant implications over urgent tasks with objectively smaller payoffs. Sort the critical and urgent jobs into priority lists. Next, prioritize significant jobs over urgent ones, as the latter are typically ineffective.

● Trim down the tasks on your list. Go over your to-do list and select the most important items (use the Covey time management grid). Establish a priority list for the jobs and activities to yield the highest results.

● Consume the was a quote attributed to Mark Twain. Take on the most significant or difficult task first; this is usually the one you will put off doing the longest and has the biggest potential to improve your life or project.

Chapter 19: Giving Workers a Voice

Establishing a strong and effective corporate culture requires employee empowerment. Employee engagement and motivation are positively correlated with feelings of support and value, which improves organizational outcomes. This chapter will examine the phases of employee empowerment and offer advice and anecdotes for successful execution.

Step 1: Interaction and Evaluation

Establishing transparent channels for feedback and communication is the first step towards employee empowerment. Giving staff members a forum to voice their ideas and grievances is essential, and management ought to be open to receiving their input. An inclusive workplace culture is created when employees feel appreciated and have a sense of belonging, which is facilitated by this communication. Giving employees constructive criticism is also essential to support their professional growth.

Create a suggestion box or feedback form where staff members can leave comments and thoughts. Organize frequent meetings with staff members to review their work progress and offer comments.

Narrative: Aravind Eye Hospital, an Indian hospital, empowered its staff in

2018 using a bottom-up decision-making process. The hospital management held frequent meetings and conversations with staff members to foster their opinions and ideas. The hospital became one of the world's most effective eye care centers thanks to this strategy, which also helped improve patient care.

Step 2: Self-Belief and Independence

The establishment of trust and autonomy is the second step in employee empowerment. Workers take ownership of their work and are more driven to succeed when trusted to finish the job. Allowing workers to make decisions about their work demonstrates faith and trust in their talents. It enables people to approach their work in fresh and creative ways by using their knowledge and abilities.

Advice: Clearly define objectives and goals for staff members and provide them with the tools they require to finish their work. Refrain from micromanaging staff members and instead allow them to work alone.

Story: By granting its employees trust and authority, the software startupGitHub empowers its workforce. Workers have unrestricted vacation time and are free to select when and where they work. Work-life balance and employee happiness have both improved due to this strategy.

Stage 3: Education and Development

Encouraging employees' learning and development is the third step in employee empowerment. Workers are more likely to be engaged and dedicated to their work when they believe they are learning and developing. Offering training and development opportunities to staff members helps them advance professionally and ultimately helps the company.

Advice: Provide staff members with regular opportunities for training and growth, such as seminars, classes, and mentorship schemes. Encourage staff members to take on additional duties and initiatives.

Story: SpaceX, an aerospace corporation, gives its workers options for ongoing training and growth, which empowers them. The organization conducts internal training programs to equip staff members with new abilities and prepare them for new positions. Because of this strategy, SpaceX is among the world's top space exploration businesses.

Problems and Solutions:

Distractions: From rowdy kids to other interruptions in the home, employees deal with various distractions at work. Establishing a dedicated workspace helps reduce these outside influences and increase concentration.

Loneliness: Employees who work remotely may feel alone and miss having in-person conversations with coworkers. Regular check-ins and virtual social gatherings can help reduce feelings of loneliness.

Balance between work and life: For remote professionals. A healthy balance can be maintained by designating distinct work hours and "unplugging" at the end of the workday.

Workload increase: Working remotely may give rise to the idea that more output is needed, which could mean longer shifts and more virtual meetings. Preventing overwork and burnout can be achieved by clearly defining expectations and priorities.

Security issues: As the use of online platforms grows, so do the hazards associated with cybersecurity. It is crucial to have strong security measures in place and teach staff members safe online habits.

The impact on family life: Women typically in charge of childcare and domestic chores may feel extra pressure from remote work. Companies should try to foster a positive work atmosphere and consider providing flexible scheduling.

Communication issues: Because there are fewer in-person interactions, some workers find working remotely more challenging. These challenges can be addressed by encouraging an environment of open communication and using various communication technologies.

Tax complexities: Remote workers for multinational corporations may have challenging tax circumstances, maybe needing to pay taxes in several nations. Remote workers can have a lighter workload if they can access tools and assistance navigating these issues.

Progress tracking can be challenging. It might be difficult to keep track of workers' advancement and productivity in remote work settings. For example, a project manager may require assistance in evaluating the contributions of each team member, which could result in miscommunications and disputes.

Some workers may feel underappreciated as a result of the lack of visibility. In contrast, others may use the opportunity to work less hard. These problems can be mitigated by implementing effective tracking systems and defining clear expectations.

Addressing and appreciating extra work. Employees who work remotely frequently work extra hours without getting paid or acknowledged. This problem contrasts conventional office settings where stressed-out workers may be compensated with incentives or other benefits. Businesses should set up procedures to monitor and compensate remote workers for overtime to ensure equitable treatment and show appreciation for their commitment and hard work.

Assessing the Appropriateness of Working from Home

After learning about the benefits and drawbacks of working remotely, you may realize that not all jobs suit remote work settings. Maintaining a fair and balanced workplace requires knowing what cannot.

Tasks Unsuitable for Remote Work

Some tasks are inappropriate for remote work because they require in-person interactions or specific equipment. These occupations include, for example, medical practitioners, transportation service providers, personnel in retail establishments, and workers in the manufacturing sector.

Employers must try to give remote and in-person workers the same perks and opportunities because not everyone can work remotely. This strategy lessens conflict between various employee types and contributes to preserving a positive work environment.

Tasks Suitable for Working Remotely

Remote work is more likely to be appropriate for jobs where the primary requirements are a computer, an internet connection, or other communication tools. The following are some examples of jobs that can be done from a distance: attorneys, writers, editors, online teachers, and data entry specialists.

A job is a contender for remote work if it can be completed without in-person encounters and just needs a computer, phone, or messaging app.

What Are the Principal Difficulties and Barriers to Productivity and Time Management?

This chapter will teach you:

● The typical difficulties and barriers keep people from efficiently managing their time and producing their best work.

● How these difficulties and barriers affect your productivity and overall health.

● A few self-assessment tools and tests to assist you in determining your strengths and shortcomings and measuring your present productivity and time management level.

What Are the Typical Difficulties and Barriers to Productivity and Time Management?

It can be difficult to be productive and manage your time. Numerous obstacles may impede your capacity to organize, rank, carry out, oversee, and assess your assignments. Several of these elements are outside sources, like:

● Interruptions: These are unforeseen occurrences or inquiries that break your concentration or momentum. They may originate from various sources, including coworkers, clients, customers, relatives, friends, etc. You risk losing track of time, forgetting what you were doing, or missing deadlines when interruptions occur.

- Distractions: These items distract your focus or curiosity from your assignments. These include social media, news, entertainment, gaming, music, noise, clutter, boredom, exhaustion, hunger, thirst, etc. They might be internal or external. Distractions might lower your level of motivation, focus, or productivity.

- Shifting priorities: These are scenarios in which you have tasks or goals that shift in response to fresh facts or events. These can be brought on by you or by other people. Examples include altering your mind, getting criticism, realizing mistakes, dealing with emergencies, handling crises, etc. You can experience confusion, overwhelm, or frustration when your priorities shift.

There are further internal components, like:

● Procrastination: This refers to putting off or avoiding tasks you know you should complete. Various factors, including perfectionism, poor self-esteem or confidence, uncertainty or directionlessness, fear of achievement or failure, etc., can bring it on. You can lose time, energy, and resources when you procrastinate.

● Overcommitment refers to the propensity to accept more obligations than you can manage. Many reasons, like the desire to impress people, prove oneself, avoid conflict or rejection, etc., may be the root of it. Overcommitting oneself might result in tension, exhaustion, or subpar work.

● Inadequate planning refers to not having a precise, doable plan for your assignments or objectives. Numerous things can contribute to it, including not knowing what has to be done, how to accomplish it, or when to do it. Other things include failing to set priorities, estimate time, divide work, etc.

Missed chances, confusion, and turmoil can arise from inadequate planning.

How Do These Difficulties and Barriers Affect Your Wellbeing and Performance?

These difficulties and barriers may negatively affect your performance and general wellbeing. Among these effects are the following:

● Reduced efficiency and productivity: You might do less in longer periods,

● with greater resources and work. You can also generate work that is of lesser quality or worth less.

● Increased stress: Deadlines may make you feel more stressed and anxious.

● Task, anticipations, or disruptions. Additionally, you might feel more exhausted or overburdened.

● A worse reputation in the workplace: You might let your supervisor down,

● Customers, clients, or colleagues with your dependability and performance. Additionally, you can miss out on opportunities for growth or notoriety.

Fewer opportunities: You might pass on brand-new tasks, difficult assignments, or educational opportunities. You might also put off pursuing your passions or interests.

● Lessfulfillment and balance: You could struggle to balance your personal and work lives. Additionally, you might have less time for the things most important to you or yourself.

How Can You Assess Your Present Productivity and Time Management Level?

In order to enhance your abilities in time management and productivity, you must first evaluate your current situation. You must recognize your advantages and disadvantages and what suits and doesn't suit you.

There are various methods to assess how productive and time-efficient you are right now, including:

● Maintaining an activity log: This serves as a record of your daily or weekly activities. You can use it to monitor your time on various tasks, how frequently you get sidetracked or stopped, and how successfully you follow through on your strategy. You can use an app, a spreadsheet, or a physical notebook to maintain an activity journal.

● Taking a quiz: This is a series of questions to assess your productivity and time management abilities, routines, and attitudes. It can provide you with comments and ideas for improvement and assist you in identifying your strengths and flaws. Numerous online tests on productivity and time management are available.

● Requesting feedback: This is an effective method of gaining opinions on your productivity and time management from people who work with or know you. It can give you fresh viewpoints, ideas, or pointers on advancing your abilities. Including your family, friends, clients, coworkers, and supervisor.

You can choose the most effective techniques and resources to assist you in achieving your improvement goals by assessing your existing productivity and time management skills.

In the upcoming chapter, we'll look at tried-and-true methods for enhancing your productivity and time management abilities. Keep checking back!

Conventional Instruments for Monitoring Goals

Using conventional goal-tracking methods may seem outdated in this digital world. However, these technologies have shown their value over time and often offer an alternative but useful viewpoint on time management. These conventional tools include the goal diary, calendar, to-do list, and token system.

To begin with, a to-do list is arguably one of the simplest yet most effective tools for tracking goals. Putting your to-do list in writing will help you focus on finishing the activities rather than worrying about remembering them all. A to-do list, however, serves as more than just a basic reminder—it also helps us prioritize and plan out our responsibilities.

It's crucial to have a to-do list that is practical and succinct. Don't give yourself too many impossible jobs or obstacles to overcome. Rather, attempt to divide ambitious objectives into smaller, more doable activities. Using "task breakdown," you can move closer to your larger objectives without feeling overburdened.

The calendar is yet another essential tool from the past for managing your schedule. A calendar lets you plan and keep track of your long-term objectives, while a to-do list is better used for tracking short-term chores. A calendar helps you see how your obligations are divided and when you will have spare time by displaying your chores and commitments throughout time.

Using a calendar can also prevent job overload and identify scheduling issues. Planning long-term projects, where multiple tasks could need your attention at once, is where this is very helpful. By planning items on your calendar, you can ensure adequate time for each task and prevent last-minute stress.

Your goal diary can be an effective tool for goal tracking, in addition to your calendar and to-do list. This tool emphasizes introspection and self-evaluation more than other tools. You may monitor your development, spot trends and issues, and remember your experiences and lessons by keeping a goal journal.

It's not necessary to have a complicated goal journal. It can be as easy as jotting down your daily accomplishments, obstacles you've encountered, and solutions. Nevertheless, even if it seems straightforward, keeping a goal journal can teach you a lot about working when you are most productive and managing your time better.

Finally, a tool that combines calendar items and to-do lists is the tab system. This method, made popular by American television writer and producer Ryan Holiday, entails writing objectives or tasks on separate index cards, which are then arranged logically.

Every tab denotes a task or objective and can be arranged in many categories or order as required. This technique is especially helpful for long-term projects or jobs that must be completed in a certain order.

In summary, conventional tools are still useful for goal tracking and time management, even though they could appear basic compared to contemporary digital apps and programs. You can utilize the to-do list, calendar, goal journal, and tab system to increase productivity, maintain focus on your objectives, and enhance time management. Always keep in mind that the ideal tool is the one that can adjust most effectively.

Methods for Avoiding Burnout

Poor time management can, unfortunately, lead to burnout, which is frequently an indication that there is a problem with our way of life or how we approach our jobs. Health in addition to impairing our efficiency and productivity at work.

Work-life balance, self-care, and mindfulness are the three main foundations of numerous burnout prevention strategies.

complete focus

live in the present moment fully, unaffected by thoughts of the past or the future. Maintaining a regular mindfulness practice can be a very helpful tool in avoiding burnout.

Meditation: This practice entails focusing on your breathing and your body's sensations while keeping an open-minded, welcoming attitude toward any ideas or feelings that surface. Anxiety enhances focus and job satisfaction and strengthens resilience to burnout.

Yoga: By encouraging us to be aware of our breathing and physical sensations, yoga helps us become more physically fit and fosters awareness. Enhanced flexibility, enhanced cardiovascular health, decreased stress, and elevated mood are among the advantages of yoga practice.

striking a balance between personal and professional life

Preventing burnout requires maintaining a good work-life balance. The following tactics may be useful:

Set boundaries: Establishing a distinct division between work and leisure time is critical. This may be setting out specific days or hours of the day as "non-work" times, or it could entail shutting off your phone or email after a set amount of time.

Quality time: Having free time is not as important as making sure that it is spent on things that truly bring us joy and rejuvenation, such as reading a book, exercising, or spending time with loved ones. that we find appealing

Individual care

Taking care of oneself is crucial to avoiding burnout. This could consist of:

Sleep: Adequate sleep is necessary for the body and mind to heal and rebuild. Verify that you are obtaining adequate sleep and that the conditions in which you sleep favor restful sleep.

Nutrition: Eating a balanced diet might help you stay happy and energetic. Eat as many different kinds of nutrient-dense foods as you can, avoiding processed and high-sugar items that can throw your energy levels off.

Exercise: Frequent exercise is a great way to combat stress and burnout and improve physical health. Whether swimming, yoga, running, walking, or any other activity you enjoy, try to fit in some physical activity every day.

Furthermore, it's critical to remember that each person is unique and that what suits one may not suit another. It is crucial to try several methods for you.

Put simply, preventing burnout entails a thoughtful, balanced attitude to life and work. It is important to take care of oneself, be present at all times, and practice better time management.

Chapter 2: Make SMART objectives

2.1 The Influence of Objectives

Setting goals is an effective strategy for maintaining motivation, focus, and progress toward your objectives. By defining your goals precisely, you may make a successful plan to lead you through the actions required to accomplish your goals. Setting goals has the following benefits that give it power:

1. Give you direction: Your goals serve as a compass to assist you in getting

through all of the responsibilities and distractions that life throws you. You can choose where to spend your time and energy more wisely if you know what you want to accomplish.

2. Boost focus: It's simpler when you have specific objectives. With this enhanced focus, you may be more productive and progress toward your goals.

3. Boost motivation: You'll be more motivated to strive toward your objectives if you set difficult but doable ones. Accomplishing a goal may further fuel your urge to pursue new objectives.

4. Promote personal development: Setting goals forces you to venture outside your comfort zone and work for

development and betterment. You will learn new things, get new experiences, and gain new insights into yourself as you strive for your objectives.

5. Promote prioritization: Setting priorities for your duties and obligations is simpler by having well-defined goals. You may manage your time and resources more efficiently by knowing which tasks will help you reach your objectives.

6. Encourage a feeling of purpose: Setting goals gives you a reason to get out of bed in the morning and face the day ahead. They also give you a sense of meaning and purpose. Achieving objectives per your principles can

improve your general happiness and wellbeing.

We will examine the idea of SMART goals and how to set and meet them successfully in the upcoming sub-chapters to enhance productivity and time management.

2.2 Creating SMART Objectives

"specific, measurable, achievable, relevant, and time-bound" are abbreviated as "SMART." It offers a structure for establishing specific, doable, and realistic goals. By utilizing the SMART criterion while defining success. An explanation of each part is provided below:

1. Particular: Your objective must be precise and well-defined, with no space

for interpretation. A clear objective answers the questions of who, what, where, when, and why. In 3 months, exercising four times a week and maintaining a healthy diet," as opposed to a general one like, "I want to get in shape."

2. Measurable: Your objective must have measurable criteria that will let you monitor your progress and assess when it has been met. Setting and achieving measurable goals helps you stay motivated because you can monitor your development and acknowledge your successes. Rather than stating, "I want to save more money," a measurable objective may be, "I want to save $5,000 in 12 months."

3. Achievable: Considering your current capabilities, limitations, and resources, your objective must be reasonable and doable. Setting difficult objectives is important, but they shouldn't be unachievable. Unrealistic goals can cause dissatisfaction and demotivation. Make sure your objectives are difficult but doable.

4. Relevant: Your aim should align with your life's purpose, long-term goals, and values. A worthwhile objective that improves your life is relevant. A related goal would be, "I will leave work on time three days a week to spend more time with my family," for instance, if you value work-life balance.

5. Time-bound: Your objective must have an end date or a specified amount of time to be accomplished. In addition to instilling a sense of urgency, deadlines can keep you motivated and focused on completing your task. An example of a time-bound objective is " within one year" instead of "I want to learn Spanish."

You may make sure that your goals are specific, doable, and appropriate for your particular situation by utilizing the SMART criteria while defining them. Consequently, this can assist you in maintaining your motivation, attention, and progress toward your goals.

Techniques for balancing work and life

Particularly in today's fast-paced, always-on world. The following tactics can assist you in striking a more favorable balance between your personal and professional lives:

Define boundaries: Make a distinct division between your personal and professional lives. You can, for instance, designate particular times for checking and replying to work-related emails. You should also remember to log off from work during non-work hours.

Make self-care a priority. Involve maintaining a healthy diet, getting enough sleep, working out, and making time for enjoyable hobbies.

Make a schedule: Make a timetable. You can plan your job hours, social time with friends and family, and time for hobbies and other interests, for instance.

Say no: It's critical to develop the ability to say no, particularly when accepting more work or tasks that would disrupt your work-life balance.

Be adaptable: Be willing to change your plans and timetable as circumstances demand. You might need to be adaptable to manage your professional and personal obligations because life can be unpredictable.

As an illustration, let's say you are a software developer working on a project that has a one-week deadline. In addition, you are a single father of two kids. Therefore you must look after them after work. You can establish boundaries by disabling work-related email notifications after hours to attain a work-life balance. Going for a stroll or working out after work. Establish a timetable by designating distinct periods for work, family, and personal pursuits. You can practice saying no by refusing to take on any new tasks that might conflict with your ongoing work. Be adaptable and modify your schedule as necessary. For instance, you can work from home if your kids have an event at school so that you can go.

In summary, maintaining a healthy work-life balance demands preparation, adaptability, and a readiness to make changes as necessary. You can discover a balance that suits your lifestyle and needs by learning to say no, establishing boundaries, prioritizing self-care, making a routine, and exercising flexibility.

Chapter 5: Maintaining Your Drive and Output

A. Determining due dates and incentives is the establishment of deadlines and rewards. Here are some pointers on how to apply this tactic successfully:

Establish reasonable deadlines: Be sure that your deadlines are reasonable and attainable. An overly strict deadline might lead to unneeded stress and hinder the completion of the assignment. Divide complex jobs into smaller, more manageable pieces and establish due dates for each phase. This can assist you in staying on course and getting closer to your objective.

Make use of a calendar: Schedule deadlines and monitor your progress using a. meet deadlines by doing this.

Reward yourself: Rewarding yourself can be a source of motivation and help you stay goal-focused. Rewards might be more substantial, like a trip or new gear, or smaller, like taking a break or treating yourself to something you enjoy.

Consider the following scenario: You are a student and have a test in one month. If you divide your study plan into weeks and assign particular topics to cover each week, you can create reasonable deadlines to meet to get decent scores. To plan these due dates and monitor your progress, use a calendar. Give yourself incentives, like a day out with friends, when you finish a week's study sessions. This might support your motivation and goal-focused focus.

To sum up, deadlines and rewards can be an effective time management strategy that will keep you motivated, focused, and well-organized. You may feel accomplished and make steady progress towards your goals by using a calendar, providing prizes for yourself, dividing smaller activities into smaller ones, and setting realistic deadlines.

Chapter Nine

Postponement in the Digital Era:

Getting through the internet distraction maze

The digital age has brought unprecedented access to knowledge, convenience, and connectedness. But technology also brought forth new difficulties, as continual online connections and distractions fueled procrastination. This chapter addresses the psychological aspects that lead to online distractions, examines the nuances of procrastination in the digital era, and guides purposefully navigating a virtual minefield.

Digital Environment: Paradise for Delayed Decisions

The widespread use of social media, smartphones, and internet entertainment has made procrastination easier. Digital devices can distract us from activities with their quick satisfaction, which makes it harder for us to stay focused and productive.

The allure of immediate satisfaction

Digital gadgets offer fast access to social media, entertainment, and information. The allure of instant satisfaction sometimes surpasses the work needed to complete tasks, which results in abdicating accountability for diversion.

The Dopamine Cycle in Internet Socialisation is

interacting with digital information. Anticipating likes, comments, or notifications creates a dopamine loop that undermines concentrated work and encourages compulsive checking.

Social Media Dilemma: Linkages against Diversions

Social media sites facilitate networking and contacts but often act as havens for procrastination. We may get distracted and less productive due to the never-ending barrage of announcements, updates, and carefully chosen information.

FOMO (fear of missing out)

Compulsive social media checking is exacerbated by FOMO or the fear of missing out on social interactions or hot material. This conduct impedes productivity and feeds the cycle of distraction.

Roll over

Scrolling through social media feeds without purpose might result in time wastage and unhappiness. The offered content frequently lacks depth and significance, encouraging surface-level participation and prolonging procrastination.

Economy of Attention: Intended to Divert

Digital platforms are made with our attention spans in mind. Providing fresh incentives and stimuli is essential to the attention economy since it encourages longer involvement, which can lower productivity.

endless scrolling and auto-playing

Features like endless scroll and autoplay movies encourage continuous engagement with digital content. Users are encouraged to spend more time on the site without concentrating on their work because of this seamless experience.

War of notifications

Announcements, purposefully crafted to provoke a prompt response, divert our attention and draw us into the digital age. An inundation of messages that never stops diverts attention and distracts the workplace.

Conscious Consumption and Digital Detoxification

It takes conscious effort to eliminate distractions and utilize digital content purposefully to foster a better connection with technology. We may reduce procrastination and restore attention control by implementing digital detoxification and mindful consumption techniques.

Digital detox: Disconnect to recharge

Digital detoxification is the deliberate withdrawal from digital devices for predetermined lengths. Cutting off. This exercise revitalizes the mind, lessens cognitive overload, and improves concentration on practical activities.

Mindful consumption: Arrange your electronic activities

Digital content selection and engagement are conscious processes of conscious consumption. You may reduce the likelihood of procrastinating and mindless browsing by structuring your online experience around your interests and objectives.

Apps for Tracking Time: Exposing Digital Habits

Time-tracking applications show trends of overuse of devices and procrastination by recording how much time you spend online. You may minimize distractions and boost productivity by making educated decisions based on your awareness of your digital habits. Among the apps for tracking digital time are:

RescueTime: An examination of digital behavior

RescueTime is a time-tracking application that keeps tabs on your online activity and generates comprehensive reports. You may create objectives, find time wasters, and develop better digital habits with the aid of this program.

Freedom: Prevent diversions

With the help of the app Freedom, you may set a time limit for blocking distracting websites and applications.

You can establish a concentrated setting that helps complete tasks by removing access to captivating distractions.

Digital Wellbeing Tools: Boost Mindfulness and Concentration

Tech businesses offer digital well-being solutions to encourage the conscious use of technology and combat procrastination, realizing the need for a balanced digital experience. Examples of these products are:

Digital Wellbeing and Screen Time on iOS and Android

On iOS and Android devices, respectively, screen time and digital well-being are built-in functions. You may set app limitations, get insights into how much your smartphone is being used, and promote better device usage practices with these tools.

Concentration mode

Focus mode lets you temporarily disable notifications from specific apps and is compatible with several devices. You can establish a work atmosphere free from distractions by minimizing the disruptions brought about by alerts.

Establish a Digital Workplace

The secret to reducing procrastination is to create a digital workspace that is free of distractions. You can work more purposefully and productively if you put methods into place that maximize your workplace and minimize internet distractions. Here are a few tactics that are highlighted:

Organize your digital area.

Arrange your digital files, folders, and workspace to reduce visual clutter. Focus increases, and cognitive load decreases in a tidy digital workspace.

Establish a focused office.

Put necessary supplies and tools on your desk to reduce visual distractions. Eliminating superfluous icons will help you resist the urge to take on irrelevant quests.

Scheduled Digital Interrupt: Tactical Activation

You may engage with online distractions in a controlled way and keep them from taking over your work by strategically incorporating digital breaks into your daily routine.

The Five-Minute Rule

Give yourself a brief respite, perhaps five minutes, to check your notifications or use social media. This deliberate engagement satisfies the need for connection while averting impulsive distraction.

grouped interruptions in digital

Plan a designated period of the day for internet contact rather than responding to every announcement. Combining these pauses lessens the jarring effect of frequent disruptions.

Partner for Accountability

Whether they are friends, family, or coworkers, accountability partners can be a valuable asset in the fight against online distractions. Keeping others informed about your objectives and advancements fosters accountability and concentrated labor.

reciprocal assistance

Assist a responsible partner in trying to cut down on online distractions. The supportive environment created by frequent check-ins and updates fosters a commitment to staying on track.

focused work sprint

Work together to take part in work-focused sprints with a responsible partner. Setting up work and break schedules in unison fosters a commitment to productivity.

Cognitive Therapy Based on Mindfulness (MBCT)

Mindfulness-Based Cognitive Therapy (MBCT) integrates cognitive therapy techniques with mindfulness meditation to treat negative thought patterns and behaviors. It is an empirically supported form of psychotherapy that can help people with ADHD become more adept at managing their time.

However, what is MBCT exactly? Fundamentally, it's a type of therapy that trains clients to be more conscious of their sensations and ideas in the here and now without passing judgment. The goal of the therapy is to teach patients how to live more mindfully and acceptingly in the now, as opposed to dwelling on the past or worrying about the future. People can learn to identify and stop harmful thinking patterns before they get out of control by being more conscious of them.

These techniques include body scans, mindful breathing, and mindful movement. Additionally, they learn to recognize harmful thought patterns and create counterstrategies to negative thought patterns, such as catastrophic thinking and negative self-talk.

MBCT also emphasizes the significance of acceptance and self-compassion. When it comes to their struggles with time management, people with ADHD frequently experience emotions of shame and guilt. As a result, MBCT encourages people to be gentle and sympathetic towards themselves instead of severely criticizing themself for their difficulties. Planning, prioritizing, and job completion can all be enhanced for ADHD sufferers by developing the capacity to control their negative thought patterns and emotions.

According to a study, MBCT can help persons with ADHD better manage their time (Schoenberg et al., 2014). The study found that after completing an MBCT program, participants' time-management abilities significantly improved, and their symptoms of anxiety and despair decreased. These results imply that MBCT may be a useful strategy for ADHD sufferers who have trouble managing their time.

Directly, lessen the impact of distractions and cultivate more constructive and positive thought patterns by fusing mindfulness practices with CBT procedures.

Workout: Intense Surfing

"Urge surfing," a strategy that entails learning to ride out urges to delay or become distracted by watching them without passing judgment and allowing them to pass without acting on them, is one of the major skills taught in Mindfulness-Based Cognitive Therapy (MBCT). People with ADHD can learn to identify when these desires are likely to happen and create ways to stop them from interfering with their productivity by practicing mindfulness of these urges. This is an illustration of a customized time-management task for MBCT:

1. Find a peaceful, cozy spot to sit or lie down to start. Breathe deeply a few times, paying attention to the movement of your breath in and out of your body.

2. Remember a recent time you had trouble managing your time. Perhaps you were putting off crucial work or were often sidetracked by social media or other pursuits.

3. Consider the following inquiries for yourself:

● What was going through my head at that very moment?

● What feelings did I feel?

- How was my physical state?

4. permit yourself to sit with these emotions and ideas without passing judgment. Realize that these are just fleeting feelings and that you can watch them without becoming sucked into them.

5. Imagine surfing the waves of your desires and impulses like a surfer. Instead of resisting or caving into them, see yourself deftly and effortlessly negotiating them.

6. Bring your focus back to your breathing and visualize yourself riding the wave of any impulse you have to partake in a time-wasting activity, like scrolling through social media. Observe

how the impulse rises and falls and finally goes, like a wave that crests and then falls.

7. Keep practicing "urge surfing" and observe how your attitude towards time management changes. You'll be able to work more intently on assignments without becoming sidetracked or giving in to the need to put things off and instead move towards your objectives.

It requires patience and time to practice mindfulness. Treat yourself with kindness and acknowledge that change comes gradually. You may cultivate a more mindful approach to time management and gain more control over your thoughts and behaviors with consistent practice.

Medication

While mindfulness-based cognitive therapy (MBCT) and cognitive behavioral therapy (CBT) can assist in managing symptoms of ADHD, medication is another option that may work well for certain people. Medications for ADHD efficiently address the main symptoms of the illness, such as impulsivity, hyperactivity, and inattention. Medications elevate certain brain chemicals that affect attention, focus, and impulse control.

Since stimulant drugs are helpful in about 70–80% of cases of ADHD, they are frequently administered as the first line of treatment. Stimulants swiftly lessen impulsivity, hyperactivity, and distractibility by raising dopamine and norepinephrine levels in the brain's synapses. There are currently 29 FDA-approved stimulant drugs on the market that use amphetamine or methylphenidate as their active ingredients. The selection of a stimulant is based on the biochemistry of each individual because various family members may react differently to the same drug.

Approximately twenty to thirty percent of people with ADHD resort to FDA-approved non-stimulant drugs when stimulant medications are ineffective. There are options including Qelbree,

Guanfacine, Clonidine, and Atomoxetine. It could take five to seven days for nonstimulants to start showing their full effects. Sustained focus, elevated mood, better memory, increased attention to detail, better sleep, and decreased impulsivity all indicate the treatment is working. These signs imply that the non-stimulant drug is having a beneficial effect on the symptoms of ADHD.

The choice of medication may vary depending on personal factors such as age, medical history, and the severity of symptoms. Both medications effectively treat ADHD symptoms (Wilens, 2018; Wigal et al., 2019). You must speak with a doctor before beginning any ADHD medication.

Although medication is a powerful tool for managing symptoms of ADHD, it may not be the best solution for all cases. While some people may have negative effects from medicine, others may not respond well to it. To choose the right drug and dosage for you.

Remembering that medicine should only be taken with a thorough treatment plan that includes counseling, dietary changes, and support from friends and family is crucial. People with ADHD can learn to effectively manage their symptoms and enhance their quality of life with the right care and assistance.

To keep motivated and concentrated, utilize visualization and uplifting affirmations.

Powerful psychological techniques like positive affirmations and visualization have been applied in various industries, including business and sports, to improve motivation, focus, and performance. These methods use the mind's capacity to shape ideas, emotions, and actions to unlock our innate capacity for achievement and self-actualization.

In essence, positive affirmations are words or sentences you say to yourself to avoid self-doubt and negative ideas. They are based on the notion that our ideas and self-talk can influence our reality. By repeating empowering and positive statements, we can develop positive thought patterns, raise our self-esteem, and become more resilient to stress and hardship.

Using affirmations entails determining which negative thinking patterns or beliefs might prevent you from moving forward and then creating positive statements to counter these bad ideas. For example, if you frequently tell yourself, "I can't handle this workload," you may create an affirmation along these lines.

Make sure your affirmations are detailed, upbeat, personal (including "I" expressions), and written in the present tense. Affirmations can be more powerful if grounded in reality and aligned with your values and beliefs.

After you've created your affirmations, apply them to your everyday activities. You could write them down in a diary, recite them in the mirror every morning, or even set alerts on your phone. These affirmations can gradually change your perspective, increase your self-assurance, and improve your drive and concentration.

In contrast, visualization entails conjuring up a scenario or mental image of reaching a desired result or objective. Similar to affirmations, visualization uses the mind's ability to "pre-experience" achievement and provide a plan for reaching it.

Visualization can take on various forms, such as imagining oneself delivering an effective presentation, visualizing the satisfaction of finishing a significant assignment or visualizing a composed and concentrated state of mind within a hectic workday. Visualizing these situations frequently might help you focus, feel less stressed, perform better, and cultivate a positive, goal-oriented mindset.

Make sure to immerse yourself in the imagined situation with all your senses when practicing visualization. A visualization might be more effective if it seems more realistic and vibrant. Similar to affirmations, regular practice and integration of visualization into your daily routine yield the greatest results.

Summarizing and positive affirmations are effective methods that can improve motivation, concentration, and output. They can support resilience, help you develop a positive outlook, and direct you towards your objectives. Regular practice and consistency are essential to gaining the benefits of these strategies, just like with any self-improvement plan. Recall that the mind is a powerful instrument that you may use to increase your success and productivity by using these strategies.

Maintain a stress-free and well-organized workstation to boost output.

The condition of your workspace can significantly affect your level of productivity, stress, and general satisfaction at work. In addition to lowering tension and reducing distractions, a neat and orderly office can promote productivity, creativity, and a sense of control. Creating such a workspace, however, takes more than simply the occasional cleaning; it calls for careful planning, routine upkeep, and the development of positive habits.

Let's start by talking about the benefits of having a tidy workspace. A clear workstation is devoid of clutter and pointless objects, which can divert your attention and make it harder to concentrate. According to research, visual clutter can impede your brain's ability to comprehend information by overloading your visual cortex. However, a tidy workstation might make it easier to focus on the task at hand, lowering stress and boosting output.

This can entail routine actions like tidying your desk at the end of the day, removing trash immediately, and wiping off surfaces to make your workspace comfortable and sanitary.

However, a well-organized workspace transcends mere cleanliness. It entails setting up your supplies and equipment in a way that facilitates your workflow and makes sense to you. This entails assigning everything to a specific location and maintaining object placement. In this manner, you can operate more efficiently and spend less time looking for what you need.

Consider using digital tools, file systems, or desk organizers to manage documents and resources. It is also necessary to keep frequently used objects close at hand and arrange related items together. Recall that the objective is to design a system that complements your unique requirements and working style. Exploring and identifying the system that works best for you is crucial because what works for one person might not work for another.

An orderly and spotless workstation carries over into your digital domain.

This entails clearing clutter from your desktop, properly handling your emails, and arranging your digital assets. It's also critical to organize your workspace's digital clutter because it may be just as irritating and distracting as real clutter.

It's important to consider your workspace's general comfort and design. A beautiful, cozy workstation can improve your attitude, motivation, and productivity. This could entail selecting comfortable, ergonomic furniture, regulating the lighting and temperature, and including unique accents like artwork or plants.

To sum up, keeping your workstation tidy and orderly is a continuous commitment that calls for deliberate effort. But the advantages—less stress, higher output, and a more enjoyable work environment—make it a worthy undertaking. You can establish an environment favorable to success and productivity by designing a workstation that complements your workflow and showcases your flair.

Chapter 3: Making Every Second Count: The Importance of Timeliness

The benefits of being on time include gaining respect and trust from others, boosting productivity, enhancing mental health, preventing procrastination and the tasks it causes, demonstrating your ability to set priorities, and much more! Being punctual is crucial for fostering positive relationships with others and reducing stress and anxiety.

It is impolite to arrive late.

It's impolite to arrive late for something. Being on time demonstrates respect for others, particularly clients and coworkers.

It's an indication of your professionalism and dedication to your work.

You convey to others that other priorities precede their needs when you arrive late for a crucial meeting.

When you go to the event venue or appointment ahead of everyone else invited, that is what is meant to be considered "on time." It is ideal if everyone arrives at least five minutes early, if possible, as this demonstrates respect and regard for others. Tell your host in advance if there's a potential that traffic may cause your arrival to be delayed by ten minutes or more so they can adapt or plan for other arrangements for those who could be inconvenienced by having to wait around for too long because someone else wasn't prompt enough!

Recall that everything in life is reciprocal! Being on time creates goodwill with bosses and coworkers, which may come in handy later on when it comes time for a promotion if someone has already run afoul of them in any capacity (but preferably not!).

Being on time shows respect and sound business judgment when work depends on it.

Punctuality is a mark of professionalism and deference. It demonstrates your respect for other people's time and your readiness to get things done. If your supervisor has informed you that they anticipate your arrival at work by 8 a.m., arriving at 8 a.m. would constitute tardiness! The same holds for client meetings and significant gatherings; it is impolite to keep people waiting.

Being on time shows respect and sound business judgment when work depends on it. If your employment necessitates consistent attendance at staff meetings or meeting deadlines for assignments or projects, for instance, being on time can be the difference between doing the task satisfactorily and facing termination for tardiness.

Teaches self-control.

Young individuals can learn to be punctual. It is a virtue. Being punctual is a skill that will help your student or child if you are a parent or teacher. Because they are dependable, punctual persons often have greater success in their personal and professional lives. Furthermore, children who often miss or are late for appointments develop bad time management skills that may persist into adulthood.

Enhances your standing.

Being on time also demonstrates respect. You are showing disdain for the person who has scheduled time for you and their time when you arrive late. Being on time should come naturally to you; if people are often waiting for you to arrive, it could be interpreted as a reflection on your character that what matters most to you at any given time is the most important thing.

We don't automatically presume that someone we have an appointment with won't show up on time; we know they will because they scheduled the appointment in the first place! Therefore, just as being stood up by someone romantically interested in us might seem like romantic rejection, it may also feel like a smack in the face when someone doesn't show up when they said they would (or worse, makes plans and breaks them).

Setting and sticking to a schedule is necessary to accomplish tasks and meet deadlines.

The things you wish to happen will require time that you have set aside. Setting aside a half-hour or so each weekend to focus on your project or planning a 30-minute block each day.

Things will never get done if you don't schedule them and write them down on the calendar. Instead, they will remain in your mind until they are completely forgotten. It can be very beneficial to set up designated blocks of time where you are not bothered by anyone and when you are certain that nothing else is going on to focus on the tasks at hand without being distracted.

Being on time requires you to be aware of the negative effects of tardiness and take proactive measures to avoid them or lessen their impact on your obligations and relationships.

More people are impacted by tardiness than simply you. It also impacts others who rely on you, such as clients, staff, pupils, or kids. Being late is reckless behavior and could cause emotional distress or even bodily harm to someone who depends on you for a crucial task, such as getting picked up from school (if left unattended).

Even if your delay is only a few minutes, taking precautions is still important to ensure your tardiness doesn't negatively impact others. For instance, departing early enough to eliminate the possibility of being late, making notes for yourself, contacting friends and/or family to remind you when needed, utilizing technology, such as the real-time traffic reports on Google Maps, to estimate travel time, etc.

Being on time has several advantages and demonstrates respect for yourself and others.

Being on time conveys your respect for both yourself and other people. It also demonstrates your consideration for others and willingness to keep your word. Being punctual is a valuable trait in both personal and professional contexts since it shows others that you can be relied upon to be on your word and to act honorably.

Being on time is crucial for effective communication, particularly when giving presentations or attending meetings. People will perceive your time as more precious than theirs if they get to the meeting ten minutes late, which may or may not be the case. People who are close to them may feel disrespected or irritated at having their time squandered as a result.

Being on time is essential to success.

Being on time is essential to success. It's more probable that others won't be on time if you're not. This may have a cascading effect, making everyone late for crucial gatherings or occasions. Being on time is more crucial than ever in today's fast-paced world.

What are the advantages of arriving on time?

● Individuals who are dependable and punctual are liked to collaborate with (this establishes trust).

● Arriving early and remaining until the end of the meeting or event demonstrates your regard for other people's time, encouraging them to reciprocate the favor.

Being on time might make you more respectable and credible to other people. When running late for an appointment or meeting, it's easy for your mind to wander. You may begin to consider the time left until the event starts and the estimated duration of each stage in your route. You're running late because your thinking has gotten completely out of control.

Use your mental energy to maintain your attention on the road ahead of you at all times rather than squandering it, worrying about what would happen if you missed an appointment. If that means getting to an appointment early or leaving work earlier than normal, do it! Recall that being on time can foster the respect and credibility necessary for professional engagement.

Your reputation for keeping your word will be enhanced by meeting deadlines on time.

You take great satisfaction in completing deadlines and are a well-organized business professional. However, did you ever consider that showing up late for meetings can indicate ineffective time management?

People lose the chance to exchange ideas, develop connections with others, and voice their opinions when they fail to be on time for meetings. Also, it conveys to their peers that they have no regard for other people's time or the proceedings of meetings if they are incessantly late and apologize for it. Should this seem familiar to you:

● Create reminders so you'll always know when things are happening.

● Pack additional clothing if needed—you never know when your wardrobe will break.

● Make sure you know where we are going by consulting a map in advance. This will help to avoid confusion.

9. Enhanced vigour

More drive and energy are the main benefits of time management. As you work harder and longer hours, your energy levels may decline, and you may experience constant fatigue.

You can control your energy and productivity by managing your time well. Enhanced vitality is one of the most significant benefits of time management. You can concentrate better on your most critical tasks when you are more energetic.

It is simpler to become overwhelmed and put off activities when one is low on energy. The most effective time managers plan their day and take regular breaks. Maintain a high energy level to help you manage your time and produce more.

10. Time for reflection

Effective time management techniques free up more time for planning and reflection. When you make a schedule for your time, you might dedicate more of it to your top priorities. If you have more time to strategize, you might dedicate more of it to accomplishing your objectives.

Ineffective time management prevents you from moving forward with your most important goals. It's not only about acting but also about considering how to achieve your objectives.

Effective time management enables creative and strategic time planning. Therefore, you might make better use of your time by being concentrated and productive.

Implications of Ineffective Time Management

What if you knew the negative effects of ineffective time management? Knowing that these mistakes could have negative consequences will help you be cautious and avoid committing them in your life.

Implications of Ineffective Time Management

1. Having trouble managing your time, which leads to bad judgments

Someone may find themselves in a scenario where they have to finish many chores quickly due to poor time management. They could, therefore, find it difficult to block off adequate time to complete chores efficiently.

People may thus find themselves in situations where they are unable to carefully consider the implications of a decision, which may force them to make a decision they may regret later.

For example, if you needed to buy a new laptop but couldn't manage your time effectively enough to get one with the configuration you desired, would you later regret your decision?

2. Confusing and Unfocused

For someone who has trouble managing their time, it might be difficult to determine how much time is appropriate for each task. As a result, he or she will lose attention. Success is supposedly dependent on having a laser-focused focus.

There exists a correlation between some impacts. Inappropriate time prioritization will lead to a person's lack of clarity, resulting in ambiguity and inattention. Ultimately, this will lead to stress, failure, not doing the necessary work to reach your objectives, etc.

If a person can't prioritize their tasks, they could miss deadlines. If you work, you are obligated to make the assignments you are given. You may need to work overtime to finish the assignments your senior or supervisor has set you.

Assume that you have decided to go on a date with your spouse or girlfriend. But due to ineffective time management, you are running late for the date. Would you be able to have a wonderful evening after that?

4. getting scared because you're not managing your time well

Consider the following scenario: You had a deadline to fulfill your commitment to your company, but you could not. You might not have too many problems if that occurred a few times. However, think about if the delays become regular. Would the job you produced satisfy your superiors? Do you anticipate receiving a positive evaluation?

Dread can be brought on by poor time management for several reasons, such as:

The anxiety associated with missing deadlines

Fear of not following through on promises or of making erroneous or fraudulent promises

instilling a fear of having poor self-worth

5. All of the stressors mentioned earlier, combined with poor time management

What else is reasonable to anticipate? One ineffective time management technique leads to a never-ending list of issues. This causes a person's emotions to begin to wane. Eventually, anxiety and stress arise from this.

Admitting you have an issue with efficiently managing your time is the most crucial step towards solving it. After the problem has been located, you can try to find its source.

After determining the underlying problems, you may focus on one small step at a time and make baby steps toward a solution.

www.ingramcontent.com/pod-product-compliance
Lightning Source LLC
Chambersburg PA
CBHW052139110526
44591CB00012B/1789